Fossils Awake

Fossils Awake

Patrick Martin

Copyright © 1989-2018 by Patrick Martin

Published by Little Whale Press
Great Cow Harbor, New York 11768

All Rights Reserved

ISBN 978-0-9801867-0-3

Cover image: "Changing Face of the North America Nebula" The North America Nebula in various wavelengths. Courtesy NASA/JPL-Caltech.

Some of the poems in this book originally appeared in the following publications:

ARK/Angel: San Francisco
Barrow Street: Gulls, Miracle Fish
Blue Collar Review: Blizzards
Boulevard: Obsolescence
The Brooklyn Review: Walking with Alison
Cimarron Review: The Restoration of Jamaica Bay (as "The Restoration of Faith near Jamaica Bay")
Excursus: Carbon[14]
Forklift, OH: Cape Cod: A Complaint, Flight
Hanging Loose: Climbing the Red Apple Supermarket
The Journal: The Trouble with Paradise
The Paris Review: The Basement, Divorce, In Dog-Years, Roaches, False Alarm
Poet Lore: Weldon Kees is Alive and Well and Living in Ohio
Poetry: Armistice Day, 1970
Spork: On Hearing Ives' 4th Symphony
Tampa Review: Garland Sarcophagus

Table of Contents

I

Armistice Day, 1970 9
The Basement 10
Blizzards 11
Climbing the Red Apple Supermarket 12
In Dog-Years 14
Walking with Alison 16
Lost Car 18
Dissection 20
Gulls 21
Pterodactyl to Hummingbird 22
Roaches 23
The Grackle 24
Counting Eagles near Blue Mountain 25
The Stars Overseeing Lehigh Valley 26

II

Cape Cod: A Complaint 29
I come to you howling and cetacean, ...30
The Occultation of Saturn 31
Carpe Aeternitam 32
I am not that 33
The Watcher, He Stops 34
False Alarm 35
San Francisco 36
Loons 37
January 1st, Year Unknown 38
Obsolescence 39

Divorce 40
Miracle Fish 41

III

On Hearing Ives' 4th Symphony 44
View from an Elevated Train 50
Beer Cloud 52
Weldon Kees is Alive and Well and Living in Ohio 55
The Middle Finger of Galileo's Right Hand 57
Garland Sarcophagus 59

IV

Carbon-14 62
Blessing at Copper River 63
Flight 64
Afternoon, at Rest 65
The Rationale for Silence at Hell's Gate 66
Hudson/Tappan 67
After Man 68
The Trouble with Paradise 69
The Climber 70
The Restoration of Jamaica Bay 71

I

Armistice Day, 1970

The porches of the three-story
brick hospital were enclosed by screens

and bars and there the veterans of the Great
War would sit in their pajamas and smoke,

slump in their rocking chairs not rocking
and wait for the nurses to take them back

to their shared rooms. Once, when it was past
the usual time, my father and I went inside,

wandered the grey halls to try and find
my mother among the nurses. She was stooped

over a man in a wheelchair, holding his wrist,
not counting. *I'll be a few more minutes.*

(He's dead.) We all waited for the doctor
to relieve my mother and write the certificate

so we could get out of the hospital, home
past two elementary schools, to our neighborhood,

where WAR was painted on stop signs
and where old men with thick glasses

waited at red lights, selling paper flowers.

The Basement

Whatever the cause, it was horrible—   the way the man on the mantle
who looked like my father died.   Sometimes, it was what appeared
on the death certificate—heart attack.   Once, a car jack

failed, pinning him under a '39 DeSoto.   When one of these stories
was told, it would stall the argument   after dinner. In that quiet,
I'd go into a basement filled   with guns and scrap lumber.

Surrounded by the cement   that held up our house,
I would try out his old   tools, to hammer things together,
to understand the grip   of those huge, wasted hands.

Blizzards

Every time it snowed, my father
   put his boots back on and waited

for the phone to ring. Already tired
   when the foreman called, he'd trudge

out of the back door and make the short drive
   to the highway garage to man a snowplow

for ten or twenty hours. He used to tell me
   how, in the middle of those nights,

he'd see lightning flash across the whole
   goddamned town. And the faintest

thunder you'll ever hear. Sometimes pacing
   with insomnia, puffing Marlboros

near a window, I've seen this, and every time
   I count in thousands like a child

but no sound ever comes.
   On Pulaski Road before I was born,

thunder was muffled to silence
   by countless acres of new snow, except

for that short tract of black
   where my father pushed through.

Climbing the Red Apple Supermarket

It isn't Colorado,
   you say but it's practice,
an exercise for mountaineering
   shoes we bought from a catalog.
Your brother the security guard
   promised to give us an hour
before he called the cops.
   I start to feel the ache
in my fingers no more
   than ten feet up: Rooves
of cars, an open dumpster.
   It doesn't look like
a parking lot looking
   down on it. You say
these are good old bricks,
   enough mortar worn away
to get almost the whole first
   joint of your fingers
between them. I say
   they're still bricks
and we're still high
   enough to break our backs,
unless we land on our heads. You
   must be crazy, you say
to think about falling
   when climbing. Scaling,
I say, it's called scaling.
   You'd shrug, if it weren't
dangerous. Scaling, climbing
   it's all up so whatever you do
don't look down.
   I do anyway, and wish
I hadn't. The car rooves again:
   can't see the headlights
from this angle. "You putz,
   I said don't look down."
A little bit of brick dust
   slips under my fingers.
I'd turn my head to shout, up

yours, but I'm too scared
to move that quickly. You
   reach out and grab the sign,
your arm not even covering
   the space inside the 'e' of
'Apple', and the sign gives
   a little bit, enough to make
you chuckle I'm almost not
   frightened when the sign
moves as I clutch it.
   I only need to lift myself
a few more times before
   the top, less terrified until
I realize this is close to
   the highest point, then we look
down from the roof.
   Garbage blows all around
the lot. Your brother
   shaking his head
at us. This is man-made
   and more steep, I say,
than any mountain. You
   say, still a mile below
most anyplace in Colorado.

In Dog-Years

Humans live
long in proportion to
what they don't

do. Lusty types
weather fast, their
skin turns to

leather before
forty. Monks
count their years

in scores,
walking robed. In
heaven, you live

forever. Comatose
humans are said to
hang on longest.

Ten years. Fifteen
years. Not long
in the grand

scheme, but an
eternity, considering
the debilitated

condition of crouching
near death. I
lived my life

in dog-years, aging
seven times faster
than needed. *Look*,

they say,
*he's twenty-three
but that's*

*one-hundred
and sixty-one
to you and me.*

Walking with Alison

Your mother, my sister, is telling
me about her new house. I've spent

so much time with a toddler,
it's nice to talk to an adult,

she says, you know? Sorry,
I wasn't listening. Every time

you point, you turn around
to our faces that don't face you.

What are you showing us?
The sunset behind the mall,

the two oaks in the neighbor's
yard, Sirius, the Dog Star,

now hidden behind a dormer?
The dozen words you know

don't have these questions in them.
Your mother tells me about the foundation,

slowly. Did you get that, she says,
clear on everything? I have time,

too much time to myself lately, as if
that was ever an explanation.

You fall down and want to be carried.
Your mother says you're a lot like me

at that age. And you throw your toys
and brood like me. I'll carry her, I say.

But you start walking again
with more care. Your mother asks you,

what?, when you raise your hand up,
and I think I know what:

Not *where did the sun go,* or *are there
owls in the trees,* but *I want that.*

Lost Car

I ask the mechanic about the narrow clearing
running parallel to the highway.

Railroad, he said. Closed since the accident.
Tracks sold for scrap during the war.

In the middle of a Tuesday night
in the winter of '37, fifty cars of coal

barreling to Montreal hit a piece of rail
twisted by freezing. Jackknifed.

Some of those cars just about flew
into the air. They say it was at least a mile

from the caboose to the engineer's head.
The rest of the crew almost froze to death

in the three hours it took to find them.
In the spring, New York Central came

to salvage what they could,
but they found only forty-nine cars.

Three shacks set against the hills,
Down the road, a boarded-up diner.

Here, this house and makeshift garage,
a half dozen auto bodies torn up and rambling

into the woods. I wonder about hamlets
like this, without commerce or charm.

When he says he's rebuilding
a '57 Plymouth, I ask why he stays here,

why he doesn't find better work--restoring
collectors' cars, or get a regular job

in one of the big garages on the Thruway.
He shrugs, throws my dead battery

to the ground, walks off to get one
that will hold a charge. I look again

into his backyard: near a trail into the woods,
a wheelbarrow and a mound of coal.

Dissection

When Science was done, Sister McMartin
would put away our half-cut hearts,
clink the padlock shut on the cabinet.
We'd recite catechisms and pray
to end the afternoon, but I longed to stoop
again over the humid, dead heart
of that kind pig and stare at its quiescent
valves, to feel the smooth,
obsolescent source of a life. I, still,
when it would it move beside me.

Gulls

                Belonging as much in a dump
       as near the Sound, one gull
swoops out an arc, carrying

a live clam which it drops
       precisely on a rock, splintering it
               to expose the single brown flesh

               called foot. Stolen
       by another gull and not
fought for. This, too,

is how they feed each other:
       not just nurturing eggs,
               the sensation like love

               felt in the spine,
       but also unceasing
bickering, the chatter

of beaks, and false shows
       of force. Elaborate enough
               to look contrived,

               they compensate for wind,
       the weight of what's in their beaks,
conversion of habitat

from one type of hospitable
       to another. They appear
               effortless enough to be

               accidental, random
       as their grasp, which
has held and dropped

everything. Do they
       wander and thrive
               and yet not comprehend?

Pterodactyl to Hummingbird

O spectacular
      blur, listen
           to your precedent,
dead and embedded

in limestone. Our young
      sang like they knew
           the names of God.
Who could guess

our food would learn
      to outrun us
           that asteroids
would bring foul air,

cool weather, and my family
      would cease. Some
           helpless, insufferably
clever creature may one day

point to your frozen impression:
      "The hummingbird,
           once called *kiss-flower*,
was the first bird to fly

backwards." I imply you;
      I am the lurch
           before soaring—
my scales transformed

into feathers—an uneasy suspension
      of belief, the part
           of flight called
failure.

Roaches

Hail the greasy automatons,   each circuit of hunger
traced on linoleum—   toward dishwater and marinara
and back under the radiator.   A commute from airless blind
walls to a sunfree   circumambulation of the sink.

Splinter-shaped, varnished bodies,   covered by flightless,
chitinous wings, they leave   a scent trail as ornate
and definite as a net. They cannot   wander. Yesterday's urges
carved their footpath. Such engines   as their impulses

are knit together like threads   into animals of every kind.
My soft, mechanical friends,   your complete biographies
are bricks from which   I was built, and in that buttery,
retreating thought is the road   to my food, my water, my solace.

The Grackle

Alarmed, the grackle stares before going.
Only sick or well-trained birds gaze

head on. This one, healthy,
wild, looks at me sideways, eye

the yellow of an old bruise. It can
smell me, not just odor in the heat

but would know, in winter, my breath:
earthbound, two-legged, clothed,

suspect and suspecting. He raises
his wings before flying to enlarge

his unrelenting identity.

Counting Eagles near Blue Mountain

The first descended and sang
into the bright gallery of the valley:
Which wind? What is my enemy?
The second, a one-eyed female
from last winter soars back now
to her one egg. Have I gone too far:
grass and sky and shallow stream? But there
rising above them all, a third, too high
for hunting, searching for new territory
and no note of me now, his figment.

The Stars Overseeing Lehigh Valley

I tell you I am near mountains and I am not.
I say I can see stars from the valley

and I am not in any valley and see no stars.
I say *you* and *we* out of convention,

even while alone, not knowing I am alone.

II

Cape Cod: A Complaint

I watch snails
make love without anxiety

or release. I do not
approve. The sea slumps

into me with a short
crest and a long, soft

crash. It sounds like *etcetera*.
Is this a promise

spoken in the language
of ocean in Spring? Or

not? The answer to that question
is the same question. If only I were

farther out on the blubbery Atlantic,
near whales' breath and *joie*

de vivre. To flop and sing
in the recondite ocean, to be

a presence that strains brine
through harp-like teeth and tastes

sugar in the salt.

I come to you howling and cetacean,

I come to you howling and cetacean,
and I sip krill slowly from a tiny planet.
I drift through the ocean, a certificate
of longing, braying, crying out plangent

monologues into the ocean, the curvature
of my spine welded to my enterprise:
O surface, open space over water. O custody
of my ribcage, a latticework prison. Envy

me my fins as I fold in silence and sing,
breathe as if I wanted oxygen and meaning
to flow within, a vivid urge singeing,
a path of anywhere I meander.

And I will treat every atom like a daffodil,
Even my skin, the pack ice, the broken daggers.

The Occultation of Saturn

The earth and the moon and the planets all
drift into each other eventually, but not that

tonight, only an imitation of that last
covering up. Cliffs behind Stinson Beach face

change in the way stones can: eternally
temporary confronting the Pacific.

outside of our lifetimes. The rings of Saturn
disappear behind some lunar craters, as if

the two were next to each other, you and I
invulnerable on the moon, watching Saturn

while a half Earth was rising behind us,
the Sun floating over our heads, blinding

but not warm, and we would wish, without air,
to be back in California, fragile, but at least

breathing in these few moments that Saturn
blinks out. On the other side of a lunar sea

of meteorites. There's candles in the pickup,
the radio, and an eclipse we can become.

Carpe Aeternitam

Your hair—
         turns white and back in sunlight.

Wait there a moment, wait
forever. We're not getting any older.

I am not that

Weird aphorisms posing grandiose paradoxes,
fantastic tricks of scale whereby my brain's
a planet you and I circumnavigate
and the Pacific a pocket mirror I twirl on its shores;

Dictionary games, synesthesia, metaphors—
Enrico Caruso hits high notes in a Model T—
lines with rhymes; rhymes looking for lines,
understatement, hyperbole, litotes, plain old lies;

They cover me like ice floes on a river:
They rise from me solid, opaque and frozen,
They are made of me. They are not me,
but they mark my movement underneath.

These trappings I wear to shed, and they bear you
myself, which I cannot wield or cast aside.

The Watcher, He Stops

On clear nights I wait in dark fields
for the sky to glow with life descending
from faint, innumerable stars. Without fear
I long for life across space's vast desert:

Some of them tall and implausibly slender,
Some reptilian with reedy, soothing voices.
They wander through galaxies like sleepwalkers,
their thoughts and flesh conjoined with void.

But Heaven, it gives only weather balloons,
marsh gas, flocks of birds, crude hoaxes.
And I blur, not a bedded rest, but a baleful
daze takes me in grass sheathed in hoarfrost.

When you and I find in each other some mooring,
for this I would trade all the footprints on the moon.

False Alarm

You can take my hand
anywhere. Tonight,
let it be the story of smoke

coming out of trash cans,
like children
making a simple plot

of escape and excitation.
We can wear masks
if we want to.

We can wear masks
if we don't want to.
But let's not ask

What we'll do
when there's no fire
and everything is turned

off, left to read under the lever,
the red, almost
understated word:

emergency?

San Francisco

*People have built a city better
than ours again.* Being from New York,
this is the one thing we say
when we go anywhere.

It's unruly; asters grow
year-long, creeping over walls. I want to say
like cancer, but I see our faces
in store windows, rippling as we walk

and I think of dogwoods
in Brooklyn, false-starting last
January, blossoms settling in slush,
fooled and beautiful.

Loons

Not just bird
        but a dismantled howl
                before it forces itself

under, wholly gone
        into the cool, dense,
                food-rich; the sound

of a world comes muffled
        through a second world, a soup
                where singular hunger

mingles with the double
        desperation of fish hearts.
                Then, repatriated

into the air, it twists
        off the lake, and if
                I must I tell this

it is with so much english
        because I thirst and slake
                in an alien tongue.

January 1st, Year Unknown
for AR

I remember a new apartment with too much heat
that I'd just moved out of. I locked the door

and slid the keys under it. There was a partial view
of the water when you sat on the fire escape.

The roof leaked into the small closets,
but it had a beautiful mantel and when

the sun rose in early spring, it put one narrow slit
of light across my face, driving me out of bed

where I might have stayed till noon. But that
was after, not long after, and I'd spent another year

not drunk, and your health looked like
it was improving and everything seemed

unpacked, and crisp snow broke
under my feet the next morning

after that party at your boss's brother's loft
in Brooklyn where I sat in some corner,

stared out a big window, talked a little to a woman
visiting from Canada. I don't remember

yelling happy new year, but we all must have.
I probably had a glass of seltzer in my hand, or water

from the sink, and I was thinking, damn, another
party where they've run out of soda. And this

is most of what I want to recall from that year
that I can't. But Audrey, if it was midnight,

who kissed us?

Obsolescence

I have been counting and cutting
forty years; I have incremented
time the last time;
today is the year Zero

Zero. The future stretches
back, yesterday the farthest.
In the other, real future, I cannot
figure; for the date, I can only put your

Name. Strangers fill your name—
my strange world, a string
of garbled characters. My mind used
to push paper, now I want my shred

Meaning. It is all over
the page. It is my pulse going
over ruled pages. It is
impulse; it is all

Over. This is my hidden object
going into the world,
the meaning of my name
divided by zero.

Divorce

Now only Venus is bright enough
to cast a shadow.

Its steady light the last contrast
before perfect dark.

Everything raised, as when
the tides wear away streets

and the curbs fall
hydrants ten feet high;

the pipes and valves
they plug into all artifice.

A place best left,
weightless, the inability

to hold down food, stomach
lining corroding—I tell this

story. I can't tell this
story. I tell this story

again. Now Venus has set. Jupiter

high in the east, its collection
of satellites like the functional family

next door. The universe sprawls,
unknown creatures, unwritten rules—

a cold, inviting city.

Miracle Fish

Curling up is for
Passionate, as the mind
around a sentence, when the words
are tangled enough.

A moving head
is *Jealous* as you lie
awake crafting
spiraling fantasies.

Flapping is *Fickle*: both
your lovers shake
hands, unaware whose flesh
they really press. *Dead*

does not move. Turning over
is *False*. I have been
dead and false
and all I could do

was turn over. If *Indifference*
is a moving tail, then why
is *Being in Love* a moving
head and tail?

My head and tail
have both moved in happy
agitation yet I do not know
what love is. O Miracle

Fish, tell me again that fishy
miracle: how I could live
as this fool and not yet
curl up.

III

On Hearing Ives' 4th Symphony
—for three voices

	Silence is the only cacophony, Charles Ives would probably have said	
A cloud of virtual particles surrounds real ones, better to describe matter as a possibility		
	as he went into the study to write music	I begin to read
occurring, or not occurring: electrons described as clouds changing shape in unknowable order,	that required two conductors, tempos shifting back and forth like clouds changing shape and shuffled manuscripts with papers calling for abolition of the Senate.	this book about Columbus, inside of which is a receipt from 1979 and a poem about love or mushrooms. (The poem is unclear.) It says *I will send spores to you.*
or knowable chaos: *Place a cat in a box with a poison tablet triggered by the decay*	Or perhaps he thought of actuarial tables, the way they tell you, with reasonable certainty, how many people	I am offended. Diamond, my orange tabby almost nudges the book out of my hands with his purring maw. The music makes him

*of one radioactive
atom.*

*The cat is both
dead
and not dead
until
the box is opened*

*collapsing the
field:*

*The event is
triggered
by the observer.*

Schrödinger's
thought
experiment

isn't strictly
accurate;
the quantum field
is
collapsed by the
poison,
or at least the poor
cat.

The point of the
analogy
is certainty

will die in car
accidents

but not who.

Sometimes, an
ensemble
sounds like it will
dominate

the music, but it
plays

in the background
and the
foreground

at the same time.

There was no
argument
in the salons of
Europe--

under the spell
of twelve-tone
music--

about the worth
of Ives' music; he
wrote
in almost total
isolation,

restless. He
knocks

over a glass on the
table
and runs away.

There was no
argument
about the earth
being flat;
the only
controversy

was the distance
to China,
which Columbus

incorrectly
calculated
as being about

three thousand
miles,
instead of twelve.
His attitude

towards the
natives
of Cuba
is monstrous.

When they give
freely,

and occurrence:
We know
how many atoms

will decay in a
    sample
of unstable
material
but not which
ones.
In isolation, one
particle

is no more
predictable
than a million as a
group.
Einstein was
offended
by quantum
mechanics

and quipped,
famously,

"God does not
play dice."
This is amusing,
considering

much of his music
premiered
decades
after it was
written.

The matter of how

Stravinsky or
Schoenberg
would have
reacted

is an open
question.
Any good student
of music
is offended by
something

in Ives. In the
third movement
of this symphony,
an organ
blasts a
monumental
chord

and is barely
heard again.
No one who cared
about the
practicality

of performance
would call

they are gentle.

When they try to
take
just as freely,
they are
barbarians.
Columbus
determined
Cuba was the
mainland.
When the natives
told him
he was on an
island,

it was proof of
their
ignorance. He
demanded
his own men not
to tell

anyone in Spain

they sailed to an
island
for fear of being
fined
or having their
tongues cut out.

Columbus
believed
he was sent by
God

the story of how
Einstein went

for an evening
walk
in Amsterdam
and forgot where
he lived.
He called
information:

*Einstein, Albert.
Ja,
die
Telefonnummer,
sehr gut...Was ist
die Adresse?*

He knew that he
must live
in one of those
houses,
just not which
one.
The map inside
his mind

for such an
instrument
and have it play

such a minor role.
Ives said he
wanted
"to hear what God
hears."

Perhaps he was
thinking
of the Mongol
archers, poised
at the brink of
dominating

all of Europe and
Asia,
but who were
called back
to the capital

never to leave
Mongolia again,
or the Vikings

who almost settled

North America

hundreds of years

before the English.

to convert the
damned
and plunder the
riches,

making no
distinction
between the two.
The authors
believe
Columbus was
kind

to the natives
(aside

from plotting
genocide),
but some of the
officers
on other ships

were more typical
soldiers.
*The captain
brought me
a native girl,
stunning
in her nudity.
When I tried

to have my way
with her,
she proved most
skillful
in the use of her
nails.*

was like a
Feynman
diagram,
all the possible
Einstein homes
drawn around a
real Albert
that walked in
confusion.

This is important,
not
because we can
see each
subatomic particle
leaving
its trail in liquid
hydrogen,

not because

humanity
is made of mesons

and leptons, not
even
because this
knowledge

has been
translated
into a mushroom
cloud.

*Watchman, Tell
us
of the Night* plays

at the same time

as *Jesus, Lover
of My Soul,* and
*Columbia,
the Gem of the
Ocean.*

This could be my
body,
with its impossible
rhythms,

and irregular
movements.

The one singing
*All Hail
the Power* might
be me.
The trombone that
plays

Joy to the World
--almost a musical
joke—
could be my
voice,

He asked
permission

of the captain

to do damage.

*After application
of the whip
she proved an
excellent harlot.*

The thought
crosses my mind:
This could be my
body,
giving in to lust
and torture,

*like mushrooms
breaking
through asphalt,*
raping,

raped, the inability
to distinguish
between

the desire and the
desired:
Powerlessness. I
am glad
when Diamond
comes

No, I am trying to talk about my body:	a place where I show up in the group portrait of the universe,	and knocks the book away from me, insisting on gentle attention,
This ineluctable particle is part of my mind, the music passing through the air.	the part of the music passing through my mind and then the air.	then biting my hands, swatting the air.

View from an Elevated Train

I sit between two families who seem
to know each other. A man next to me
is staring at a set of new, identical keys,
lining them up, as if his eyes were pins
in the lock. Bored, I wonder: an apartment,
padlocks? Yesterday's *Times* is on the floor.

A pillar of smoke in the distance.
We stop at 74th St. I imagine the bright saris
facing the street: even saris imported from Japan
with mirrors sewn into them. Indian desserts I
can't pronounce. One family gets off.
A woman sits next to me and immediately

opens the U.S. Citizenship Practice Test.
She circles *Thomas Jefferson*
just before I turn away. The burning
building may be one of those high-rises
in Woodside. The doors close.
Not many people get on at 69th.

Still a few empty seats. Across from me, twins
who are not dressed alike. One asleep
on her mother's thigh. The other playing with a toy
cell phone, tired, cranky. The air
acrid. Fire engines from the street.
I reach and close the window. We stop

between stations. The woman with the test
stands to look out. Someone comes in
from the next car with a guitar begins to sing
in Spanish. His voice not gentle but his playing
skillful. A ballad. It must be
the side facing away that's in flames.

Should see fire by now. *Oro*
is the only word I can understand. *Gold:*
So much more beautiful in Spanish!
Like the Latin command *Ora*: pray.
The woman with the test is crying,
I think, as she looks out. No,

it's dust. It's one of those tall buildings
right on Roosevelt Avenue. We're moving again
for only a few minutes, when the train
pulls into Woodside, almost knocking a boy
into my lap. Although avoiding it, I meet someone's
glance. He looks for a seat. There are none.

Beer Cloud

"Using one of the world's largest radio telescopes, British scientists have analyzed an interstellar gas cloud and calculated that it contains enough alcohol to make 400 trillion trillion pints of beer."
                The New York *Times*, May 30, 1995

Why beer,
      the first spirit
   to be drunk...
            what possessed people
      to concoct it?

                                        More strange
                             than melting ore
                                but a much older
                  craft. Before metal,
                        without plows,

pouring water
      and hops together
and leaving it...
            That's the strangest
     part, the waiting:

                                        Brutish, yes,
                                   but not nasty.
                                   Patient. We always
                       imagine our low-browed
                             ancestors as desperate,

dumb, plagued
      by baboons and
bad teeth. Frantic,
           not leisurely makers
     of beer, who gazed

                                                  into each
                                 other's eyes:

                                        the animal tending
                                 most towards
                                    intimacy: affection

so great
         their brains split
into words.
                  They would face
            each other

                                                 and cluck
                                         their sharp
                                              tongues, laugh,
                                  imitate the wilder
                                         animals. I wish

I could
       go back and
talk to them,
              Upright posture, I'd say,
        great idea.

                                                Thanks again
                                           for leaving
                                                the trees. They
                                would run away
                                          back to their

children
         and beer.
I'd watch from
              the brush as they pointed
         into a night sky

                                                    dark as
                                 Guinness and made
                                         the first constellations.
                          The same chemistry
                                 that made them.

We see
       beer a cloud

1,000 times the diameter
        of our own solar system
    because we have evolved

                                into bartenders
                        and astronomers.
                              What if there
            is life stirring on some
                      green planet
in that cloud?
    Creatures like us,
but not people,
        who have bypassed
    or perhaps

                                surpassed
                      being human.
                         Do they look
            up (can they?) into
              their boozy sky and see

no stars, only
    a warm glow,
like the feeling
        of a stiff drink in the gut
    I hope they

                                can journey
                        out of the vast
                              murk and
              see what I see
                now, and ask:

    How many eyes? How many empty mugs?

Weldon Kees is Alive and Well and Living in Ohio

The driver's license you bought in a shady part of Columbus
says *Chris Weldon* and I've seen you wince
when a busboy calls you by your last name.
Just Chris, you say, a shiver in your voice, more
than a desire to be unceremonious. Everything came out
when we got drunk after work and I said hell,

let's drive to Cleveland. I know a jazz club open till six
where every other drink is free. We can pass out
in a cloud of smoke, by the low shuddering of the bass.
Excitement rippled across your face
and died. *I might be recognized*.
I thought you were a murderer.

I can guess the details—car parked by a bridge,
long walk to the bus station—, but I don't get
the whole point. It seems like a meticulously planned,
pointless crime, only explains how you seem restless,
but taciturn, why you cringe when there's a broadcast from the
    Apollo
and turn the radio off. We feed families of six, truck drivers,

and when you stand among the tuna melts and chicken
    sandwiches—steaks
the size of dinner plates, dinner plates the size of hubcaps—you
    seem
absurd, lost, as if you had to eat all that food, as if you were
    watching
all the meat, fish and vegetables you'd ever consume
being served these good corn-fed citizens. *Roost and roast
in the flames.* You shake your head. *It's enough to make one
    go on a diet.*

Before cashing out, you disappear into the alley
for a quick smoke. Watching you stare
at the garbage cans, before I knew your last name
was your first, I thought you were one of those men
who never recovers when his wife leaves, or the single survivor
of an unlucky platoon, a man who lost his soul,

not discarded it. I often start to ask you about the old life,
some story about the blues and reckless living, at least a poem.
But I stifle myself before speaking, a gesture,
I suppose, I caught from you. Your life must be like the lull
between lunch and dinner, after the nooners leave, anticipating
the customers who come to take an ordinary meal. C'mon Chris,
tell me about the unbearable music, and the silence that follows.

The Middle Finger of Galileo's Right Hand
--Institute and Museum of the History of Science of Florence, Italy

"...the illustrious hand covered the heavens
        and indicated their immense space,"
            but it's just the finger, and probably not
the one he pointed with, except

sometimes, excited, livid and joined
        to a jointed, living forefinger, waving,
            incessantly correcting some patron's
mathematics, like an angry saint awakened

and walking out of a hermit's cave, or the ruffled
        brother who awakened him, saying, "Old fool
            come back to the monastery.
You'll be eaten alive by snakes

before Christ leaves His throne to answer you."
        Prophetic, incorrigible, crabbed, this finger
            scratched the hairline of his wrinkled brow,
as he peered at the 'ears' of Saturn, and tugged

at the waist of his faded, ill-fitting doublets.
        If Galileo came back and saw us glaring,
            he would just want that finger again; his
spirited corpse would lift the glass

and take this beloved, desiccated digit
        from the house arrest of its glass case
            and hold it still in the lately animate,
trembling right hand, and it, too, would tremble

as it found its place in the empty socket,
        amid forefinger and ring, the old familiar
            opposable thumb opposing
the strength of the prodigal, withered tarsal.

"Why not a finger for every city in Italy?
    a lump of flesh for every town?" All
        around him, a stunned crowd
of tourists. School-age children

from London, Beijing, and Rome.
    Perhaps someone would call out, "Signore Galilee…"
        before he looked and walked through us all,
His gaze straight, like light. His back bent, like light.

Garland Sarcophagus

Roman, circa A.D. 200-225, Metropolitan Museum, New York

"The back and cover of the sarcophagus are unfinished, and its inscription is blank, which may imply that it went unsold in antiquity."

In one of those last dread works, Eros
awakens Psyche with an arrow
and they embrace. They bear

the body with perfunctory solemnity,
towards the unmarked graves
on one of the less illustrious hills. His final

sculpture uninscribed, not worthy
of being buried—poor Blautius,
such a bad salesman, and worse,

he couldn't even finish that last
grave jar. Night falls. Mourners revel
in an infinitesimal victory: All of Rome

has outlived another casketmaker!

IV

Carbon-14

It must be the warmest summer
in ten thousand years because
the beast has been worked out of the glacier
with whited eyes turned inward
and a stomach still full
of sweet flowers.

It began earlier even than this,
as a tunneling itch
in a puddle, a cascade that
turned itself into taxicabs, ice cream
and two figures in Pompeii, caked
in powdered obsidian, same as they were
when their mountain exploded.

Run fur past the Geiger counter
and sense its prime element,
black and pure. History
is a countdown, a march
of half-lives receding
into the future even as we take
our place in its exploding clock.

Blessing at Copper River

May night find you knocked
off your little mountain

of mind, into the valley below the iceberg
that cools seashells snapping

in half beneath your feet. Let that dark
curl around you like a lapdog. Beyond

your vision: hunters. Thunder
from the east horizon. Go to the water.

Drink deeply enough, you may find there
the flailing spirit that drinks you.

Flight

In the clouds I think
I wish and forget what
as they expand and darken

as we fly into Minnesota. I'm cold
and the baby in the next aisle
has fallen asleep. The woman

next to me reading
The Stand closes the book:
it's almost time for me to close

and sleep. The woman looks like a queen
in a rowboat. She can't bear
the trashy book, the clutter of steerage, *I wish*

is what I was thinking, the darkening
turning into clouds, expansion
flying to Minnesota. The cold baby

has me falling halfway to Minnesota,
and I just might ape the clouds,
expand and wish as I cry and clutter.

Afternoon, at Rest

I walked my hands from the Sonora to the Gobi.
Oceans raked under my fingernails.
The shadows we made spun

under the dome of my puzzled head.
I couldn't sleep on the plastic sheets
or cope with exercising on the lawn.

I bathed in flickering light until
I could see you, fading globe,
still spinning where I caressed you.

Did anything stay awake with me?

The Rationale for Silence at Hell's Gate

The Manhattan skyline without a memorable building:
    Roosevelt
Island, halfway there, managed by a single corporation. Uniform

housing beside the rubble of a sanitarium. A towering complex
of pipes discharge a broad gush into the river. Two crossings:

a railroad trestle and the Triborough. The trestle soars more;
dingy, sand-colored arches line up a mile before the shore, like
    a nave,

framing part of Astoria Park. Nothing green under the shadow:
four-family houses embraced by the monumental, uninhabitable

concrete. Trains rumble far above an arbitrary pace.
Call it Hell's Gate because the confluence of the East and
    Harlem

traps small craft while tugboats push late at night
garbage scows through the impossible water. Waves roil

and break in the middle of the rivers, but the tide plays out
finally into whitecaps that cannot reach the shore.

Hudson/Tappan

Rainwater and melt, it starts from the mountains,
an aimless stream. These last thirty five winters
no thaw brought it over its shores,
nor have these summers seen the riverbed.

Twice a day, it inhales, it surrenders to the harbor.
It brings eels out of their slumber, the hybrid
life of ancient and brackish, it carries freighters
from the hinterlands to the breakable skyline.

My mind has grown double like the river.
Like the currents, it extends, it grasps,
a moving duplicity of falling and rising.

It sings brackish and brown: it contrives
to be a harbor, an inland sea. Where it forms
it goes, and where I am free I double back.

After Man

When forests have overgrown the ruins
of the last pyramid, and the last sailor forgets—
windswept, without a port—his sextant,
and against the levees the ocean strives,

the tarred-over ground will pull up a green,
living blanket, and bridges warp and tumble
into their unmarked rivers, and the free,
newborn world fill with harmonious breathing.

But vine meets briar in prehensile apprehension
and the eagle's nest becomes an archive.
And crickets sing the night in Cantonese
while grasshoppers answer in Mandarin.

And wherever two living things contend,
there they dream us up, and we live in them.

The Trouble with Paradise

I remember walking over a railroad bridge near
    Interstate 610 in Houston.
It was the middle of summer and I was breathing
    exhaust and humidity.
Between the ties, I looked down at a fifty-foot drop
    to a dry stream bed.
Traffic crawled along the highway towards the rice towers
    that were being demolished.

The sun disappeared behind the towers and I realized
    it would never set that way again:
These towers eclipsing the sun in early evening, seen
    from a railroad bridge in August,
Me crossing that awful bridge for the last time, grumbling
    and wanting to move back East.
I don't miss it. I wasn't happy being on Earth in the end
    and I couldn't wait to leave Texas.

Paradise is a lot like Paris, I thought the first few millennia,
    and dead Parisians agreed.
Floor to ceiling, the place is crammed with art. The streets
    are always being cleaned,
And people are so friendly. But the angels have their ways
    of making you feel uneasy,
Even when they're being polite. Take your time, they say,
    because time is all there is.

The Climber

I would like to tell you
that I went easily
or that, hand over hand,
the way was steep and

Mysterious, but I stopped
often, cursed my stylized
tennis shoes, the contents
of my bag—too much food, no

Water. I was passed
by the wind and other hikers;
it was simple untreacherous
work which I did like an

Ant. I cannot tell you
how long this has been going
on; something splits me—it's
the air not working—no

Voice; it's my legs, a ringing
in the bones, my will
diminishes, like decomposing
granite, the map is my only

Power. At the summit,
the water in my voice rises in me
like an ant, like a power in this
mysterious mountain.

The Restoration of Jamaica Bay

I'm not supposed to be here,
on the other side of the sign:

Bird Sanctuary, within earshot
of Kennedy Airport. My father

can remember when it was
Idyllwild, when LaGuardia

was Municipal, before jets.
Eggs are everywhere.

This was once the time of year
for Canada Geese to migrate.

In parks, they might attack
but here, they are afraid of me,

not the low jets. There were hawks
living in the Pan Am Building

thriving on pigeons, reconciled
with the helicopters, but wary

of window washers. Two cranes
fly low and land with unlikely grace.

A plane comes in so close I can read
Lufthansa on its tail. It startles

only me. They call it Kennedy to make
one man live longer, but the concrete

won't go on forever, and without steel
or thoughts: Hatch and alight.

www.ingramcontent.com/pod-product-compliance
Lightning Source LLC
Chambersburg PA
CBHW051715040426
42446CB00008B/893